T0326861

THE**OBVIOUS**

New Issues Poetry & Prose

Editor	Herbert Scott
Copy Editors	Lisa Lishman, Jonathan Pugh
Managing Editor	Marianne E. Swierenga
Assistants to the Editor	Rebecca Beech, Christine Byks, Kevin Kinsella
Business Manager	Michele McLaughlin
Fiscal Officer	Marilyn Rowe

New Issues Poetry & Prose
The College of Arts and Sciences
Western Michigan University
Kalamazoo, MI 49008

First Edition, 2004.

ISBN   1-930974-47-7
Library of Congress Cataloging-in-Publication Data:
Paul, Bradley
The Obvious/Bradley Paul
Library of Congress Control Number: 2004102394

Art Director	Tricia Hennessy
Designer	Carmen Johnson
Production Manager	Paul Sizer
	The Design Center, Department of Art
	College of Fine Arts
	Western Michigan University

THE **OBVIOUS**

BRADLEY PAUL

New Issues

WESTERN MICHIGAN UNIVERSITY

Writing with restrained clarities and precarious meditations that characterize late Stevens and Ashbery, Bradley Paul thinks through days, presenting freshly slant realities, bringing mindfulness into and through each line not in a linear way but unpredictably as consciousness, geometrically. These appealing poems have strong and vast dictions; they discover words and linger with them in original, comradely ways.

—Brenda Hillman, judge's statement

for Karri

Contents

Acknowledgments

Acknowledgment is made to the magazines in which some of these poems have been published:

American Poetry Review
Boomerang
Boston Review
Denver Quarterly
Fence
Fine Madness
Gulf Coast
The Harvard Review
Iowa Review
Interstates and Serious Lakes, a limited-edition
    anthology published by O. Press
Maryland Poetry Review
Sonora Review
Third Coast Review

Many thanks to friends in Baltimore, Chattanooga and Iowa City; I'd like to particularly thank Karri Harrison Paul, Richard Jackson, John Yau and D.A. Powell for their extensive assistance with various aspects of these poems.

"If one draws a map without having graduated divisions, there is no means of distinguishing between what is near and what is far . . . But . . . a true scale representation of the distances is fixed by the graduated divisions. So also the reality of the relative positions is attained by the use of paced sides of right-angled triangles; and the true scale of degrees and figures is reproduced by the determinations of high and low, angular dimensions, and curved or straight lines. Thus even if there are great obstacles in the shape of high mountains or vast lakes, huge distances of strange places, necessitating climbs and descents, retracing of steps or detours—everything can be taken into account and determined."

—Phei Hsui

I.

first Teeth; Width

To Paraphrase

I invoked one thing for questioning;
all things were ripe;
I remembered the taste of just one food;
it was May when I ate it
and I was sick on that day,
yet all things were ripe
and festered on the pavement,
the mulberries and the musk-rose
and the heavy other fruits.
And the moss came up from the bricks
and tasted each thing once
and for a long time.
And I knew about this
and spoke not to the ear
nor to the steaming grass,
and did not look at the pear on its bough,
and tasted no thing for any time,
and felt no settlement of the heavy air,
though it was the thing that I wanted.

And All This Time We'd Believed in Oxygen

Give it a light, this little Coleman stove.
Its body has been porcelainized
and the porcelain has started to chip.
A person might curl as the twilight does,
shaved above the meadow. Far back
on the pocked terrazzo, old Lucretius
explains the nature of porcelain:
as they gather on the side of a hill
the chips shift a little in the wind,
and that makes them look like a herd of sheep.
Their sheep's heads sag with so much plodding,
and the latitudes out here bend, stressed
and thin at their stitches.
The shepherd makes his way across the moors
where you and I sit with our frying tins.
Night begins from the ground up.
The sheep graze with their eyes closed.
The shepherd must think they're asleep
so he lies down, and his own hunger
starts up. How thin is this earth's shell!
His hunger starts up, and is dark
with white little stars.

Rectangular Hole in the Living Room Wall

It was eleven inches wide
and half as high.
It was very calcified
from where certain water
passed through. I mean,
its corners were grained over
and they were like the shells of oysters.
We were delirious and maybe
pathetic to sit beneath it.
Waiting, just waiting, as if
the water would come again.
Then sleep, hard and white.
Buried in halves somewhere near,
like an oyster shell,
with pounds of water
laid on top.

The Timely Performance of Duties

Tiling the scrap-wood kitchen
for my mother, for religion,
for Order and its tray of spoons—
I, Pipes-Outside-The-Wall,
scraped like a plate across the garbage pail,
stupid, something, tired,
said the page or two
I know how to read
is English smally written on a plate,
Thy salt and thy cart
are northerly bound, the ice
held by number 8 screws—
Our little God over us everything lords,
He purples the 8-screw world
where do we everywheres inquire
and is, my friends, in his houndstooth lovely—
I read it clearly, thought, Come on, Pipes,
come unlamped up,
within a year of the century
your President died;
so what. Look at your plate.
Thou maketh a woods
with thy English-on-Plates
and the firs stand up therein.

On Humidity

To leave by the storm door
is something, and hot,
the illegible sun and the vandalized tree,
the tree with three trunks
and the overwrought ferns.
A plastic cup is caught in the breeze . . .
One passes the tree.
The tree is something.
There is a stop sign, loose rivets,
and the neighbors blare—
it's not even nine—
it is disgusting air.
The ferns drop.
Go back inside;
turn the aluminum blinds down.
One turns down blinds.
One is fat, and the cord is dark brown.

Instructions on Weight

Thin your body.
The knees and the back
must bear less.
There is foam
between the bones
that wears.

It's not a machine, you know.
Not a metal one.
Observe its holiday.
Populate the village
another day.
Save the devil masks
for a later carnivál.
It finds walking
redundant as rain.
Refrain, refrain.

At the First Roulette Table

Thirty-eight was the number they gave
to anyone interested in a number.
It was about technique.
So the fluttering of bare numerals
would lie still when the county came to tax.
The grass came up around the abandoned helicopters
and then the grass went down.
It was summer—so the leaflets said—
and that's when things got cluttered.
Thirty-eight was the number they gave.
There was no devil, no reason,
and the paper angels had been taped
and remounted on the voyeuse.

Written in a Time of Average Rain

Briefly conifers, and mud
at noon minutely.
A little man on a large blue hill,
the blue as is common in Norway.
The stone gives itself a name
at the funnel-bottom
of the massive day:

People Looking at a Photo Album

We were animated around the photograph,
like birds, like birdseed
falling on the sidewalk.
Our retreat was episodic,
an all-out stupidity, yes,
though our assumptions
were not as plain
as those we had learned
and the scenery stalled
from one year to the next.
That's how it was with trees and so on:
stray locust, ruptured seed,
a dog with fish nearby.
I would say the light
—the light stumbling on obtuse objects,
the light on the brick
and the fertilized field—
was not what we wanted.
So we repaired to another room
and in that room the radiator slumped
to the cracked wall behind it.
There was a broken tumbler,
and the scent of the redbuds
was fresh along the sill.

The World is a Fat Place, and Its Seasons are Small

So I thought behemothly of the waltz in the tree.
The sun in threes unfurling.

Instructions on Macbeth

Smidge the forest a smidge to the left.
Nail it. Good. Again. It's leaning.
Or is that you? Whatever.
At least now we can see.
The castle is center.
Look at the stones,
the turret, the goat
chewing quaintly by the gate.
The snow assumes
the tilt of the granite roof.
It's wonderful. Everything's wonderful.
Tell the actors, Ready.

II.

Parts, with annotations

Reconstructed Landscape in Summer

I began in the middle for things
were immense and begun:
rain was immediate
on the sycamore leaves;
the calm animals entirely
were aggressive and bright
and the entire land was ripe
and had the exact look of being ripe.
Not even the obscure night was dull
nor even was the thunder vague
despite my own large breaths, my
mumbling shouts to friends ahead,
irate as a bucket of forks, yes, but
muggy, invisible, approximate, and slow.

What Is Here and Why
—a missal

Smoke.
Here to nettle.
It is true they give me blue to wear.

I am the foreign army
here to bide in the woods.

A poster to announce
their uncatholic aims.

Many people,
to make death thorough.

A massive noise
makes our body stop.

I believe we should kill their country.

Winter is erected
leaf by leaf.

The phone book from that other decade
to demonstrate how your parents dialed.

A large red letter
to emphasize the chapter's start.

Squares with numbers
to efface this most pathetic year.

Impress of one-time words
to indicate what the monks removed.

Yellow dims your reading.

Unwieldy doubt,
here to drone.

Family,
to thieve,
and for whom I grieve,

green wax
to lade with poison,

the act of allotment
because of the wine,

a beast that is content indoors—

the angel leaves
his spot in the hierarchy.

A great oculus
sprawls above the pilgrims.

Landowska
masters the harpsichord.

Anon and ere,
so thou might archaicize—

it is all so wonderfully great,
wave to the people, wave!

At Bimbo's Broken Note
or Why They Don't Let Me Prep for Satchmo Anymore

The boss, black bulb, jangled—"make
now, hurry, uh, a microphone

check—" "—but Applehead," I said,
"I've never," and paddled for a bung,

but he sunk me an "aw, sport, give
it a whiz," and'd already

surfaced to the production room;
so I stopped myself, and uncapped

the pearlies for a run-through gurgle
and wheeze, and the vast blue (in

those blue lights) cabaret seemed
to me to (slivered) shimmy

like the coined wet bouffants
that deeply numbered in (steeped

deep in fifths of hooch) the house
lights night into night. I could

have cored myself, him, in such
gravity was I a nickel shy

of breaking his dime in half,
I budded like a sappéd man

in my one-two-one-twos,
plucked before my bones were right,

heavy-seeded and sour
in my barrel, deaf,

green, rhumbaed through and split,
and sobbing in slides and clicks.

Frantic Lights, Terminal Lights: The Man Who Invented Paper

Paper was made because Tsai Lun
said it should be made.
He was adamant, like a fable,
yet vague, like a fable.
The rabbit asked "Why?"
and "In what city?"
and as the blanket proffered its answer
everyone said "You're a blanket,
stop talking." Inane,
peregrine, all those things.
All was bright
in the bay window's yawp:
that is how I remember our street.
The bricks were brown
and the sidewalk was plugged with elms,
like Tsai Lun saying
"We didn't know it would be light green,
but we knew it would be a moth."

Why I Left Nepal

There are some lakes in Nepal that hate me.
I think, "Nepal, how you do terrify me to the quick."
I lie down, as one might, in a lake pink with evening.
It's as if the seasons might begin,
a very black bird growing blacker in the sky.
The size of a nickel, then the size of your hand,
darkening toward your eyes.
Friend, you are fat unlike most people.
You lie down in the pink lake
and it's as if the seasons had begun.
Crabs roll in all the water you displace.
I am mashed into pearl, parts of me,
and parts of me into tar.
The trees darken as if your brow were vexed.
You think, "Nepal, how it does frighten me to the quick."
There are tea leaves under your right thumbnail
and tea leaves under your left.
Goats move across your ribs.
A gang of shoats nips at your reeds.
They dig for the truffles they love.
"Obese," say the arboreal saints,
agreeing among the eucalyptus,
"as the daylight that fills Nepal."

Mao's Melons

First we get the damn pagodas.
Then the little pagodas they put the crickets in.
We hang those on the huge red willow
at Xiang-pei, and then get some sleep
or crawl around in a sleep-like manner
under the huge willow. We crawl
among the egrets. In dumb egret fear
they startle. We crawl to the creek
and get some honeysuckle or some lilies,
and some of those big watermelons.
Christ, those melons are big.
They are without precedent.
History pares out their seeds on a cool day
and the wind yaps at its side.
Crickets wrench their way
into the melons' pulp.
On a cool day History leaves the creek
with skinned toes yawning.
Long leaves slither on the yapping wind.
O salt of my willowed skin! we want those melons.
It's like a bastinado to eat one, little workers,
and the egrets start awfully inside you.

Regarding the Natural Portrayal of Persons

To follow thistles white
beneath the white orchard
crowded with blue immobile birds,
to think of lagging houselights

across the swimming pool
I was an idiot, and grateful
as idiots are, and unhurried
by the screendoor's harried

swing. It was someone new or less
to crowd our memory of the fruit
lying for three days in the grass.
Three spots of soot

spread on the leaning apple
till the apple
leaned beyond its wasted shadow.
Then voices as though

the muscular lake were thawing
and the grass were ripe and long—
they had gotten the colors wrong
though the orchard was nearly done.

Lament for Giovanni, Brother of Guglielmo

Why is my alligator so tame? I bait him
with orchids and aquiline pears;
I solder his scales and vaccuum his teeth;
I buff his muzzle with an undarned sock.
He is aquiline and wicked smooth.
He is invisible in the pear orchard,
where he buoys down like a petal.
Floats on down, and his laps are unkeened
by the mistempered air.
Perchè non si arrabia? my friend
would say. My friend, Giovanni Marconi,
who is likewise smooth in the profile.
He is a well-wired little tube,
though he suffers in his headphones,
crawls inside one of his headphones
as if it were a tractor tire
and rolls through the rows of trees,
gnashing and rumbling his heart-styled spleen.
Giovanni, cut out that racket!
Get out of that orchard, and into the pond.

Homage to Edvard Kocbek

Mud blisters the ditchman's face and
in the ditchman's syke lies the quacksalver
who stutters with his tonics through a dream.
A Russian wastrel basks there
in the dream's rotting and earnest hay.
His name is Pasha, which means Little Paul.
In sleep he dines the debutante whittling
spoons outside the Croatian cabaret.
A drunkard sucks the grass at night.
The tenor pipes down by 4 a.m.
The preacher seals the tenor's fife with beeswax.
The miser accounts for the preacher's lesions.
On a panel of the beehive
has appeared the horoscope,
the farm boss reads it with a marten's blink.
The hayracks had been green in May;
that is, they'd been racked with hay.
The hay is home to vermin.
The vermin fall like cabbage from the dream.
The dumb cabbage snickers downriver
past the moping cuckold.
He'd been suckered at the cala farm
and lilies fan flat around him
and the bank is somewhat pristine:
like all slapdash hell
did the silver nitrate blacken with light.
With dented cups in the soupline
do the bums wad my sleep and ken.
I have mirrors on my shoes.
Light gets trapped around me.
It's like I'm happy, music
slides kicking onto the deck
like the dolphins dumped
from the miser's woven net. A lunar vista

is stenciled on the dropcloth behind it.
In crater-light and flags did I try to speak:
the heart therefore lies stupid in its water.

Blurbs for Hamlet

"Poulet would have it that the future is a woods
peopled upon utterance with rhododendron etc.
Our speech when we speak of 'to do' or 'will be'
tosses nominal seeds among the misoneistic ferns,
ferns of course of happenstance,
whereon the aphids themselves are corrupt.
Tame the woods we might
with darkling pansies and vineling plums.
Our will to sow is itself a weed."

"Surely the rhododendron has procured a berth
among our unfeeblest flora."

"Hamlet's blue chalk thinking
suggests billiards more than architecture.
'—Billiards indeed!' might depone Laertes."

Mistaken Regard for the Objects in Starnle's Basement

Ah, the Classics.
Starnle loves the Classics.
In a versatile but focused way.
As if ruddied in a beet jar.

Aha, he will change his name.
To Breath-of-Baby-Jesus.
To Bilked-Beside-a-Pine.
To Hour-and-Twenty-Minutes.

And then the drawer
beneath the mitre bench.
A wrench, a nickel,
and a cumbersome belt.

Now why does Starnle have that bench?
In the basement with the limestone walls
and the uneven floor
and the shelf with the cherry preserves.

On Humidity

"Insomnia Lays its Blue Tracks
into the TV"
I titled my first mural.
"Blue Do the Pistons Go"
was the next.
I showed them to the Mexicans
Orozco
and Diego Rivera.
These two. I tell you what.
A tangelo had petrified
in Diego's pocket
and it weighed just an ounce.
It was smaller than a lime
and you could imagine the channels
tight inside it.
When the wall tightened
and Diego said "Leñador"
I knew he was quoting Lorca.
When Orozco said
"The stirrups of my ears"
he was in pain.
His face was that of a scaffold being upended,
a scaffold pushed out from the bottom,
and the worker's lunch flies everywhere.
Orozco turned from the mural
called "Blue Do the Pistons Go."
"Quickly," he said,
"I must show you my new mural,
on the side of the auto parts store."
What awful cars they had in that town.
That town was like burning cork.
Orozco was in real pain.
We wanted to help him, Diego and I.
We bought some pistachios,

a quarter pound,
unsalted,
and walked with him to his mural,
called "Sun. Trachea of the Sun. Water."

The Coliseum

Enrico Fermi was a physicist,
he taught physics in Rome,
limited subway, little bronze
she-wolf, suckling bronze sprats,
which word comes from sprouts,
the spring lettuce still frozen
like Vespasian said, "Let's build something,
people, we might as well."
Then he came to Columbia
and that was that; the silvery chocolates
lure us back into the street,
the ground breaded with tar
and the tar breaded with stones.
"Are you a pilot or are you a naturalist?"
asks the proconsul, and answers himself
"Africa, O Africa,"
and things begin to grow. Once
they had a city,
camels et cetera;
now they have a city,
camels et cetera,
four-dollar cokes, rancid birds—
it is loose, said Enrico,
so add an egg, add two eggs
and whip it around. That man
in Campo dei Fiori
is on fire and is waving.
Into smoke he squeezes
like a Fiat through the monger-laden square—
Who would have said it?
Their language sounds like scissors.
Their scissors sound like a wren
or something common
treading at the far side of the pool
where the gallies oar up for a fight—

Look, a plastic straw, the straw's wrapper,
the little bit you did not drink—
the arena stupid with morning
and saying "People,
O People, where are you?"

O, My Skin! *or* Morning in Corniglia

I slept in the fiberglass,
it was pink,
I dreamt of the urchins,
they waited,
and of the nearly fresh inlet
which had in it a limestone jetty
and an Italian swimming man
and I called for the restaurateurs
who were arguing above the inlet.
I ate the plant they told me to eat,
it had thorns and a spine yet was not a cactus,
I thought of a man,
he was angry and said Get up!
and the first thing I saw
was the orange Frigidaire
and the limes that they grow now
in Liguria, salted with the air's
salt. I ran along the lines,
I was lanky and common
and my skin was common
and black, the sun upright
on the upright Ligurian sea!

Noah Remembers the Coast of Senegal

Came the list finally, though without
its rotting apple or its vinyl sheath
of miniature ivory elephants
nor the wood on which they leaned
nor the sand they remembered to traipse—
they could get nothing done at this pace!
If fish were brought up they were brought up
with kelp and garbage and sand.
Some still breathed in the brutal nets,
some were blue and some green
like the ferns left behind in the heat;
some were dark like the ants on the fern
or the darker ants moving down the fern
away from the blackening trees.

Seventh of Twelve

Truthfully, the Minotaur usually slept.
The centaurs had a still
and were getting to be quite savvy.
They had to live here too
so they kept things toned down.
It was only while the Poet was here,
they said, "Keep up appearances,
Poets talk!" And unless he saw
some real wages-of-sin spectacle,
some truly woolly-bully penitence,
we were liable to get real supervision.
"He'll likely look a long time.
Poets like to let things sink in.
If he asks you anything
make like you're real sorry."
Also they brought in a bunch of Italians.
And indeed he looked, but was nervous
and missed a lot.
He had to ask twenty
before one would say a thing;
others taunted him
just out of earshot: "I've
got three soupbones here
and guess which dog is getting them!"
He fiddled with a human eye
that had been placed there for effect
but didn't seem to register what it was.
Ribs stuck out of the ground
and on these he scraped his shoes.
They said he was plainspoken and democratic
but plain people don't speak as he did
nor do they wear such shoes.
He took some notes, he poked at the walls,

and his friend threw a fit for a ride until
Nessus carried them off. He would have
anyway. Then they turned the lights back up.
Saltines were passed around
to help with the nausea.
Many crawled out of the blood.
But a few lingered near the massive radiator
for it was still quite hot,
and they guessed at how this heat would be described.

Thumb Sliced Open

It prattles like glass but deeper.

The color of your voice
moves in me.

The Incantations Native to The House Etc.
in Which One Resides

I'm in Germany, which is bad enough
and the new Turkish busboy is holding to me a pencil
and pointing dumb to a pad
so I say *bleistift* but write *pencil*
and he looks dumbly to me
so I say *pencil*. The pad is sort of pink.
Later he brings me some milk.
The cowbells squawk outside on the pines.
I think "Archduke" or "chipped-off granite."
It's difficult because I've just come from Turkey
through Slovenia, which is the sunny side of the Alps.
My host there came on to me at the Okarina or the Steklenica
and then skipped out on the check.
He may be drinking Union Pivo now.
He may be drinking it at Prešeren's statue
and coming on to more Americans
since this is a tourist hotspot.
And why not? It's a great statue of quite some bronze.
Still, I love the Slovenes.
They are the salt of Europe.
They are the reason Austria still has an economy,
foul schilling. They are Austria's raison d'être.
My grandmother because she kept books at Amrhein's Bakery
claims to know German.
She also goes yearly to the German biergarten
in downtown Baltimore,
or just outside of downtown
in Pigtown, and frequently sees Erma Smith
though Smith is not German.
One year Uncle Freddy showed up in lederhosen.
They were blue with silver horseshoes pinned on.
This is no surprise if you know Freddy.

People said, "Lederhosen, how perverse"
or "Oh god, lederhosen"
or "God" or "Jesus"
or "God and Baby Jesus."
The apertures snow takes on during a rainstorm.
I miss the nave at St. Stanislaus.
I miss the rowhomes
hedging the glassy streets.
There is blue glass
sealed into the streets.
It gives ridiculous traction
to errant Fords and so on,
so that the Fords don't slam into Chevies
and thereby become Chevies.
The glass is blacked over by winter
and salted free by spring.

Description of the Salt Cellar

Copper alloy with garnet clenched to.
The salt green-collared.
Casual like a small country.
With a matching inkwell that brays.

How do you regard error?
With a burro's face.
Did the salt taste of the cellar?
Metal was on my tongue.

I sat down to eat:
the tomatoes were red.
I meant with stubborn color
to write your name.
Salt that lopes
like ink from a copper well.

Not Lazy But Despondent Over the Status Accorded Hunting Dogs

So the hunting dogs aren't happy.
I suppose, then, that they're miserable,
though Misery becometh not a hunting dog.
The sages say Misery is like a bobby pin
wrangled among the lint of a wastebasket
in the laundry room, and how long
since the concrete floor was painted?
Though the sages are not laconic
they are content with feta and olives
on their roughened limestone patios.
Their quarries must have been drawn from nothing.
Look how blue the water is.
Yea, Misery pointeth with a capricious humour.
I have eaten so many pins
that they form a trap in my stomach.
I am therefore hungry.
Even olives will not go down.
This is ridiculous policy.
Does your beehive unravel?
Once there were some dogs.
Their pen was decrepit
but they did not hate bobby pins
such as the ones I had swallowed.
I've eaten a lot of pins.
They starve me.
They want to be my constitution.
I dreamt I ran to the cinderblock building I knew
on Beechfield Avenue,
the beauty parlor,
and coughed and drank rapeseed and bicarbonate
and the pins came out.
They flew everywhere in this parlor,
behind the vertical aluminum blinds,

into the helmets of the hair-drying machines,
then dropped to the linoleum's fleurs-de-lis.
They looked up at the drop ceiling.
Styrofoam.
"See, pins?" I said,
"I loved you, so I brought you home."
They said, "Then why do you dream about dogs?"

Betoothed (A Turn in the Italian Manner)

Pipes laments his feta teeth
and in his plaint they crumble more.
His walking flesh shirks
the palliative sun.

He is compelled to sugar
and sweats it.
In the lines of his every bandwidth
he sees it is No Good—
he gargles, must,
with a gargoyle's bilge.
Sleeps with draining teeth.
Awakes to a body

he does not like,
curses, curses;
Pipes' skeleton cannot bite.

Goodbye to Adjutant P'ing T'an-Jan

Over—oh steep—those mountained hectares—

Who has silked any decent path?—

Where P'an Ch'ou hauled his books and dog—

Where insomnia laid its dark blue tracks—

The pear trees blacken in the thinnered heights

And the flutes are horned with grousing.

By a year's wide thumb does one tread the Gobi

The rivers plotted like forks on its yellow face—

In hardly a season will those attachés learn

To sip our rice wine and our dumb pear brandy—

Our pear brandy steeped in Yüeh-Chih's skull—

On the Day of the Revolution

Slight, and sprigged, and pinked
like a just-green yew, heartsick and mined

—I panicked when our wrangled trees
were pinched for snuff (the

punkwood navy had gone to pot!),
I lowed when our snuffiers were pasted out—

with the teeth of Order busted
(I forgot my heaven sown

in hedge-rowed skies, who wouldn't?)
and its throat unjeweled of its wedged-in

quartz (I cursed those mountains
with their shaved-down stumps to boot!)

orioles scared from a thatch of pikes
(a random dog sniffed around for fat—)

and the stars were scored and gauged in their stalls
(and mashed his pelt in the mis-cut earth.)

The Business of Central Maryland

My coke was watery.
I almost Visa'd the tarnished forceps
and vague calipers at the vintage store
where the proprietress had me coin
her nearly flagged meter
and I liked her voice.
I put $8
on two football pools.
The common victor
was the Green Bay Packers,
my brother's team.
I met Lacey the Chapter 8
from near Tennessee;
his colicky son
interns for the Sun
paper, is a freelance plumber
and sometime beachcomber,
"the sun doth roughen
in the sea's expiring brine."
After four hits
from my Ventolin asthma inhaler
every byte of air
was a spiral in my lungs.
I phoned
unsuccessfully
Jeffrey, Lauren,
Big Daddy, Meghan,
and Robby, though Robby's
girl Lisa answered,
said she and Robby
were splits,
Evil Ted
is gay.
I did speak to Karri;

Karri, my stomach is filled with corduroy.
You are not spiralled
on the blue divan.
Downstairs the furnace
rushes, stalls,
and pennies out heat
by its irresolute little
ongoing meter.
Clarinets hang in my eyes.
The TV stalls.
When I go with Mikey
to the Eagles game,
section 752, row 10,
seats 18 and 19,
we'll go early
for parking and nachos.
We'll amble to
our nosebleed seats
and wait for the football's stupid yardage—
the clocks reset and run—
stuttering and tripped up by penalty.

View from the Amphitheatre

There is so much light
that nothing seems different.
The walk, as white

as the grass, and the elderbugs,
pixels of white.
The chorus has fixed on this

and is popular
for our hearing is wide
and attentive. It is

True Nature, in that
it happens all at once
but seemingly toward a point

whereon you weather
among a kill of lilies.
Yet there ticks the strain

of a rain-logged rafter
in the actors' pens nearby,
and the popular chorus

adjusts its masks of Concern.
The petals fill
the blinding sky

but the pistils,
meant to depict decorative
people, darken.

A Small Variety of Beachcombers

I slept there.
It was hammocky
but without the swing.
I do believe I did not swing.
A green fruit above me
made a shade.
A dog strolled in, and lay,
then a graceful upright mantis
in supposed prayer, in this shade
red. The shade was slightly public
like the swimsuit tents
in this increasingly touristy town,
and passersby sensed
a person in sleep,
a head full of tumbling plastic bottles,
the shade full of bottles
under the green fruit,
its green rind taut with sharp seams.
Here, take one home with you.
It gives a buoyant, tumbling shade.
It is the new kind of beach.

Pick a Color to Describe to a Blind Person

Black: is what I think you see
in the rear-window view of the church, orange,
and the steel that cables aright its spire, weak,
because it moved eight blocks in the war
because the Yankees wanted to burn it
and the South wanted to burn it
and melt its bell
into ten minutes of mortar.
In its floodlights the bats are blue
then yellow then quickly nothing,
like the mosquitoes they chase,
like the green moths or the moon
toward which they list,
like the hungry who come
for the intermittent food,
the birds and the roots
that old ladies cook
and half falls into the sewer,
is thrown into the sewer
and drains to the Chesapeake Bay
snagged in grass and eaten by slime,
completely wasted, totally wasted.
Or *White:* the black I think you see is wrong.

Answers to Chapter Six

Because the camel ate an apple, she ate an apple too.
The sugar was fast in her brain.
She said, "disrepair."
Because the copper was spent.
She was at Leon's on Tuesday.
Two oranges and a block of cheddar.
Because I think she was dreaming.
She sat up and the light bulb was beside her.
The patio was slick.
She was there long enough to meet the suicide.
She walked because the choke wouldn't catch.
Limes were on the counter.
Her friends were unreasonable and arthritic.
They found things possible.
Because she felt heavy.
Reluctant in the window and reluctant in the door.
Reluctant in the stairwell where the angel hung.
Reluctant above the dogwood branch
confused by a reluctant March.

Instructions on February

But March has no hurry in it.
The copper cornice faster greens.

A laughter of snow considers its melt.
A haggle of cars takes up its creep.
There was the thing they said they thought about,
verdant water, a shout, a bark,
glass vial in the tread of shoe,
it clacks underfoot for a block or two.

But not in this stuttering now.
The stupid world wears its muff.
Eventual is its niftiest pace.
A failing fog ahems.
Shovel.

New Instructions

Put weight atop
its meagre gravity.

Passersby
have something to say.

Press your brother.
He'll make you angry.

Even the miniature pines
comment.

Someone complains
it's the sitting itself

that the yellow windows hear.
Will anyone regret this loss?

A face that looks like letters.
A chime as sharp as tinsel.

It blares through even
the grain of old film,

as strange as paying money
and as strange as anger

that I remember
in only a few, clear moments.

Who will live this briefly?
In rapid, empty

pictures. Briefly,
so that we can see how.

The Obvious

Pipes who does my speaking
does not appreciate a name.
But he speaks with spillage and burn.
Each of his porous teeth unscrews.

The advice he follows is to salt
his tongue and his gums.
He so licks the earth
that a crater forms

with rain at its bottom so thin
it cannot be swallowed.
Oxygen has a thicker cloy
and more animals in it

eating and swimming in tiny skins.
The air has more of an animal smell.
Pipes who speaks for me
destroys his favorite plastic plate;

he sets his index cards aside
and opens his mouth and sleeps,
and feels as though he has never been
hungry, or in need of water, or sleep.

III.

third Teeth. *or*, Animals who Matter

Instructions on the Brain

Enter a word or phrase.
If you're not sure, guess.
Be specific.
Something close, something similar.
And use less memory.
It's more efficient that way.
It's faster.
Friend. Shape.
Alley. Mouth.
The streetlight orange behind her.
The orange of her breath unfurls.
Now I remember. Now I remember.
Something green is in the room.
A moth. A voice.
The man is happy.
Her smell is on the pillow still.
I remember now. I am sure I want to quit.

A Chapter from *Speeches I Avoid*

Eulogies. Never.
Did he deserve death?
What's "deserve?"
The stale flowers cloy
and the small cards
with name and saint
tilt.
One lament described his name
"suffixed no more to our complaint
nor prefixed to our whim."
Look at us, flaunting our language
over the breeds that piss outdoors.
"He was loved":
true or a lie, we already know,
but it's more saleable than the other points:
his gaudy aspect of papier mâché
turns orange and limp
like an onion rotting in the alley.
His fumes and tissue sort
like plastic letters
pulled from the felt placard.
His genius and battery dimmed,
the swishing bag of gas and acid flattened—
who wants to be the guy
pointing out that, hey,
we're all molecules, basically?

Look at us, flaunting our language
over the breeds that piss outdoors.
Eat the fauna
or leave it alone!
Otherwise, he had a brick rowhome
painted several greens.
Let's flip it now and call it a capital gain.
The title tax is worth comment
and the 1041 and the Schedule D,

but his eulogy,
cloying, reiterative, stale,
is just a draft of our own.

Lessons Regarding the Work

Moreover he made an elm of it.
He made also a month
and the month disrupted the elm.

Now, the elm drew up what it touched
and it was air, and people, and water.

And the month lived in the air and was air
itself. The air appeared as twenty-seven houses
and in them grew the elm.

Yet the elm stopped in the air. So the houses stopped
and the air stopped in them.

He altogether made the air. The elm
was disrupted with air, and from it fell the month
and many months, and from these months

fell what you'd expect from months made of air and houses:
an elm, and mistakes, and time.

Your Semi-Arcs Sliced and Reflected

You threw low with the vigor of
a thrush caught in a fusebox or
a strange belljar blown
from the pigiron left molten
by someone in the furnace
while they pleaded with
the floor boss whose say
is bound by surely nothing
invented during that one
harsh winter, you know,
when those dollied men had their
moving and December stooped
straight down to the basement
window, where we had a
ball of a time, garnishments or not.

An Animal

It was bright. It was riled.
It sang inside an empty bottle
and so was green through it.

SPCA

She loved her crate,
the mix giving me
whites-of-eyes,
intent on sleep
and kenneled away
from the stress-whining
others. The kittens lowed,
the arsoned raccoon was raw,
the pound ran low
on sedative.

This dog soon mine
had blood made a sludge
by heartworms
and skull a pumice
by earmites,
dangling dew-claws
and three-hundred dollars' worth
of mange, and a security deposit
of anxiety chewing—

but in two months
it was all undone,
"She just needed quiet."
Further description
superfluous seems.
Now the dog plays well,
is affable,
comes home to kibble
then kennels promptly away
in her steel and pillowy crate,
faithful but direct, and so on.
You've had a dog,

maybe culled metaphors
from the trot and routine.
But what conceits you breed
neuter themselves
because the dog uses only
a small set of words
to be clear on how the pack works—
Enough, Quiet, Bring, Move Over,
what people want.
People want much.
Of course she loves her crate.

On Waiting for K to Take More Things to Goodwill, UPS, Etc.

It may be a while. It may be a while.
There is yet little to do.
Little might stall and unstall
with the bend particular
to your hand in sleep—

          Regarding her time
my friend was nearly certain.
My friend was nearly certain regarding her time—

it is a small room, ours,
and there is yet little to do.
Of cedar it smells
but less and less.
It widens at the windows (the light
is less than it was);
it reddens the body
of a particular cheap lamp
and the lamp gives its drawn-out pall.
Had I seen it enter at all?
July is slow. My friend, I expect you.

Orioles vs. Chicago 9/11/96

In my stomach it might be one of those hopeless innings,
the ball hung foul on a fragile nail
two-hundred feet above the sense
you and I make of the field, the chalk, the wall,
and the numbers plucked
from the ground's waiting breadth.

On the Circumstances Regarding Our Business

Prayer, I said a little one,
Deferential, I was,
among the huge red casks of olive oil
and the skidloads of salt and dried basil.
Expensive our shipment
and late for my brother's barge,
I had a stopper for the cask
and a little brown rosary—
bread, I had a slice,
I'd have liked it with a dish of oil.
Oil with a dish of salt.
On the nicks and shambled body
of my thumbworn Christ
I said a little prayer:
"Oil, be slow. Be oil,
and do not sink—
wealthy make us soon."
With fury, my brother pressed,
and the casks were heavy to move.

On My Mother's Wall Carpet of the Last Supper

Fall. Remember. Sleep
which is Fall and Remember.
See colors of whom names
are differently twelve. Yet
so blind I am silver
and nearly a coin
and man who absorbs
nearly coin.
That their faces all
are undifferently worn.
But look. You may regret.
You may also mortar
and make palatable. It is
a round window; it is
a zero unto the garden wherein
are twelve too many sounds,
and they are particular.

The Atlantic Ocean is Green

I love the Atlantic because I know three miles of it
that like an atlas spoke and opened in grids
and widely beckoned to the bulged-out night

as though it were a bees' hive full of wrens;
and I died at the tip of my breath
who in the stagnant ocean tread

beyond your ken, and in the breeze
one heard a plastic bag. The roots of the beach grass
show above the sand. However swollen is one

is how undone the next, the winter, I think:
The blue umbrellas beside the grass are gone
and the gulls among the darker birds are thin.

Also There are Flares

For Hell has many codes, one two,
they are unusual.
For the dog is the beginning
and counts.
For dark recurs, one two one two;
and in boxes one two
keep we blacking.
For in breath is blacking
and pause; and in pause
we are heard, one two
one two, though in blacking
is pause set afoot.

And the Evening as Well

Pipes' skull. Plate
is Pipes' memory. *And* right now

the neighbor drinketh a drink
of water, *and* people look

and, Pipes, your cant is
sparrow, sparrow, little else—

Possession

Who put a window in these several walls
meant for men to enter,
meant for the Zenith and the RCA
to be temporary, teeth that needn't
knock long in their gum.
Technology becomes an abscess.
It means a pause
to the man who comes to fetch it;
the parquet nicks
beneath his drag;
the flotsam remains
that will not sell.
It is not worthwhile to have no things
but only happenstance if you do (too
many stores of immediate pawn
crenellate the many streets
to verify notions of "have" or "hold")—
the television is here to talk a while,
is all, and to consider the room
with its oblong light.
It channels the rather picturesque,
now towns of ruin
whose turrets tilt with pock,
now former planets whose coldened sun
crumbled to dumb hurtling meteor.
The spaces through which we fall
are for now nearby.

Among Architects

But the windows, KINGLET, are *square*
and the light is *flat*
and will flatten *everything*
for Photography hates a *breeze,*

crumbs in a fan-shape *fallen:*
the Hen is *bland*
and walks in *weeds*
and above her GARDEN is *terrible,* thin—

I Say Pint Because Pints Can be Measured
and Because We Hover Above Our Measurements.
I Say Hover Because That's How Water Looks.

So the slick bird twisted in its happy pint
and bird-blinked in the water
in the bronze lily above the living lilies . . .
I assumed it was a grackle, and that
it had rained a little, and from these errors
had at least a notion or so:
It climbed above the summery tires
and made surveillance;
It was abreast of it all as a spider
is abreast of the ceiling;
The tin cans were amassed and waiting
and even the asphalt was sweet.

But what I meant to take
was given from the get-go.
The grass declines its summer sheath
and every nerve gripes to its stringy end,
just as on our mythical stones
and as though we'd never read them.
Never read He walked, or He had
another use for Every, and his Pace
was in That. He took frantic leave
and was purple in his innermost leaves.
He was for one second black on the black statue.
And he numbered his conches for sale.
Now we walk outside and are too weak
and sweating. We hang like keys by the door
or flap our tinny flap. Slowly,
I intended to see you,
and stood with a snowcone by the gate—

There should be one season per day and each one
numbered, as in a thorough and thoughtful
concordance. You in your blue jacket
can be seen from blocks away. Once
I lost the page for fruit, and everyone was angry
and clopped on. I thought of the Philistine
with the wrench, how tired
he and I were and flecked blue
by floating billiard dust:

The city is taut among the verdant rest of it.
Houses snap along the block and come
to a jaunty end. They said benzene
is heavy in the clouds
and we asked what benzene did.
It works in twos, was all,
and with my ticket I walked up Charles
to the Wednesday roast
beyond the abruptly priced
Marlboros and upon the heavy grates. Until
we were in nothing but the foil
and upright alien splints.
We called it an Orchard
and in a phone booth the spiral lamps
made rapid breaths above us.
The grocer's voice, but not
in the aisles as usual—

They all suggested the glass
but the glass was the most sinister thing
and white among the grass.
As if it were culled from an ethery cellar
like the panels from a finale

to which we made adjustments.
Dinner plates bright along a vine,
each person with a synchronized watch.
Each one sighting friends over several days
though distance drapes their arrival.
Our friend bares his cigarettes
and they are white to us,
slicing and miniature,
and the lachrymose dog beside him feeds.

Instructions on Pornography

> *If, to go from A to B, the characters are taking longer than*
> *you would like, then the film you are seeing is pornographic.*
> —Umberto Eco

The bottom is the bottom line but
along the way are flowers.
Such white flowers on such a beach
among such sharp fanning grass.
How scalding is the sand
beneath this step, then this, then this.
Read between my teeth, she says,
which seems provocative,
then talks at length about TV,
how here it is red,
here yellow, here green.
He says, That certainly is TV.
Loud, too.
This sand is certainly white.
People in California are nice.
Flowers, and grass, and TV, and sand.
The fucking's in the uncut walk.

Notes

Epigraph: Phei Hsui, a Chinese cartographer, was appointed Minister of Works to the Chi'n Dynasty in 267 A.D.

"To Paraphrase": "I spoke not to the ear" and the "musk-rose" are references to various Keats poems.

"And All This Time We'd Believed in Oxygen": cf. Lucretius' tract "De Rerum Natura."

"Lament for Giovanni, Brother of Guglielmo": The Italian phrase means "Why does he not grow angry?"

"Homage to Edvard Kocbek": Edvard Kocbek is a Slovene poet from the early 20th century; the poem is based on his poem "The Game."

"Blurbs For Hamlet": cf. Poulet's essay "Vauvenargues."

"The Incantations Native to the House Etc. in Which One Resides": "Union Pivo" is a Slovene beer. Prešeren is Slovenia's great Romantic poet. Uncle Freddy's blue suspenders with silver horseshoes are attire for a fan of the Baltimore Colts.

"Goodbye to Adjutant P'ing T'an-Jan": This is an adaptation of a Wang Wei poem with the same title.

"Pick a Color to Describe to a Blind Person": The title is taken from the essay section of a local art school's application form.

"Orioles vs. Chicago 9/11/96": The Orioles won this game in the eleventh inning, when Eddie Murray's long fly ball allowed Rafael Palmeiro to tag up and run home.

"Instructions on Pornography": cf. Eco's essay "How to Recognize a Porn Movie."

photo by Karri Harrison Paul

Bradley Paul is a poet and filmmaker living in Baltimore. A graduate of the University of Tennessee at Chattanooga and the University of Iowa Writers' Workshop, his work has appeared in numerous periodicals, including *American Poetry Review*, *Boston Review*, *Iowa Review*, and *Fence*. Paul also wrote and directed the independent feature film *The Monstrous V9*, and his screenplays have received several awards. He has spoken at numerous conferences, including the International P.E.N. Conference in Slovenia, the Meacham Writers' Conference and the Conference of the Baltimore Writers' Alliance.

New Issues Poetry & Prose

Editor, Herbert Scott

Vito Aiuto, *Self-Portrait as Jerry Quarry*

James Armstrong, *Monument In A Summer Hat*

Claire Bateman, *Clumsy*

Maria Beig, *Hermine: An Animal Life* (fiction)

Michael Burkard, *Pennsylvania Collection Agency*

Christopher Bursk, *Ovid at Fifteen*

Anthony Butts, *Fifth Season*

Anthony Butts, *Little Low Heaven*

Kevin Cantwell, *Something Black in the Green Part of Your Eye*

Gladys Cardiff, *A Bare Unpainted Table*

Kevin Clark, *In the Evening of No Warning*

Cynie Cory, *American Girl*

Jim Daniels, *Night with Drive-By Shooting Stars*

Joseph Featherstone, *Brace's Cove*

Lisa Fishman, *The Deep Heart's Core Is a Suitcase*

Robert Grunst, *The Smallest Bird in North America*

Paul Guest, *The Resurrection of the Body and the Ruin of the World*

Robert Haight, *Emergences and Spinner Falls*

Mark Halperin, *Time as Distance*

Myronn Hardy, *Approaching the Center*

Brian Henry, *Graft*

Edward Haworth Hoeppner, *Rain Through High Windows*

Cynthia Hogue, *Flux*

Christine Hume, *Alaskaphrenia*

Janet Kauffman, *Rot* (fiction)

Josie Kearns, *New Numbers*

Maurice Kilwein Guevara, *Autobiography of So-and-so: Poems in Prose*

Ruth Ellen Kocher, *When the Moon Knows You're Wandering*

Ruth Ellen Kocher, *One Girl Babylon*

Gerry LaFemina, *Window Facing Winter*

Steve Langan, *Freezing*

Lance Larsen, *Erasable Walls*

David Dodd Lee, *Abrupt Rural*
David Dodd Lee, *Downsides of Fish Culture*
M.L. Liebler, *The Moon a Box*
Deanne Lundin, *The Ginseng Hunter's Notebook*
Barbara Maloutas, *In a Combination of Practices*
Joy Manesiotis, *They Sing to Her Bones*
Sarah Mangold, *Household Mechanics*
Gail Martin, *The Hourglass Heart*
David Marlatt, *A Hog Slaughtering Woman*
Louise Mathias, *Lark Apprentice*
Gretchen Mattox, *Buddha Box*
Gretchen Mattox, *Goodnight Architecture*
Paula McLain, *Less of Her*
Sarah Messer, *Bandit Letters*
Malena Mörling, *Ocean Avenue*
Julie Moulds, *The Woman with a Cubed Head*
Gerald Murnane, *The Plains* (fiction)
Marsha de la O, *Black Hope*
C. Mikal Oness, *Water Becomes Bone*
Bradley Paul, *The Obvious*
Elizabeth Powell, *The Republic of Self*
Margaret Rabb, *Granite Dives*
Rebecca Reynolds, *Daughter of the Hangnail; The Bovine Two-Step*
Martha Rhodes, *Perfect Disappearance*
Beth Roberts, *Brief Moral History in Blue*
John Rybicki, *Traveling at High Speeds* (expanded second edition)
Mary Ann Samyn, *Inside the Yellow Dress*
Mary Ann Samyn, *Purr*
Ever Saskya, *The Porch is a Journey Different From the House*
Mark Scott, *Tactile Values*
Martha Serpas, *Côte Blanche*
Diane Seuss-Brakeman, *It Blows You Hollow*
Elaine Sexton, *Sleuth*
Marc Sheehan, *Greatest Hits*
Sarah Jane Smith, *No Thanks—and Other Stories* (fiction)
Heidi Lynn Staples, *Guess Can Gallop*
Phillip Sterling, *Mutual Shores*